Anonymous

The Inauguration of the Rev. Francis Landey Patton

As President of Princeton College

Anonymous

The Inauguration of the Rev. Francis Landey Patton
As President of Princeton College

ISBN/EAN: 9783337171308

Printed in Europe, USA, Canada, Australia, Japan

Cover: Foto ©ninafisch / pixelio.de

More available books at **www.hansebooks.com**

Princeton ... ...

THE

INAUGURATION

OF THE

REV. FRANCIS LANDEY PATTON, D.D., LL.D.,

AS

PRESIDENT OF PRINCETON COLLEGE.

————

Princeton, N. J., June 20th, 1888.

I.

Order of Ceremonies.

II.

Address on behalf of the College,

By Rev. JAMES O. MURRAY, D.D., LLD.,
Dean of the College.

III.

Address on behalf of the Alumni,

By the Rev. HENRY VAN DYKE, D.D., '73.
President of the Princeton Club of New York.

IV.

Inaugural Address,

By PRESIDENT PATTON.

SERVICES AT THE INAUGURATION

OF THE

REV. FRANCIS LANDEY PATTON, D.D., LL.D.,

AS PRESIDENT OF THE COLLEGE OF NEW JERSEY,

WEDNESDAY, JUNE 20, 1888.

PRESIDING OFFICER

HIS EXCELLENCY ROBERT S. GREEN, LL.D.,

Governor of New Jersey.

The procession formed in the campus in front of Nassau Hall at two o'clock p. m.

GRAND MARSHAL, SUSSEX D. DAVIS, ESQ., '59.

Order of Procession.

1. The Governor of the State and the President of the College.
2. The President-Elect and the Chancellor of the State.
3. The Officiating Clergymen and Orators of the day.
4. The Trustees of the College.
5. The Faculty of the College.
6. The Trustees, Directors and Faculty, of the Princeton Theological Seminary.
7. Invited Guests.
8. The Alumni.
9. The Fellows and University Students.
10. Alumni of other Colleges.
11. Undergraduates.
12. Citizens.

The procession moved as soon as formed to the First Church.

Order of Exercises.

I. MUSIC.

ORGAN PRELUDE.
Chorale—Veni Creator Spiritus.

ORGAN, ORCHESTRA, CHOIR.

II. OPENING PRAYER,

The Rev. THEODORE L. CUYLER, D.D., LL.D.

III. ADDRESS ON BEHALF OF THE COLLEGE,

PROFESSOR JAMES O. MURRAY, D.D., LL.D.
Dean of the College.

IV. ADDRESS ON BEHALF OF THE ALUMNI,

The Rev. HENRY VAN DYKE, D.D.,
President of the Princeton Club of New York.

V. MUSIC,

EIN FESTE BURG,   Martin Luther.
ORCHESTRA, CHOIR AND CONGREGATION.

VI. ADMINISTRATION OF THE OATH OF OFFICE TO THE PRESIDENT-ELECT,

HON. ALEXANDER T. McGILL, JR.,
Chancellor of the State of New Jersey.

VII. DELIVERY OF THE CHARTER AND KEYS OF THE COLLEGE TO THE PRESIDENT-ELECT,

The Rev. JAMES McCOSH, D.D., LL.D., Litt.D.
President of the College.

VIII. INAUGURAL ADDRESS,

The Rev. FRANCIS LANDEY PATTON, D.D., LL.D.
President-Elect.

IX. MUSIC,

THE OLD HUNDREDTH PSALM.
ORCHESTRA, CHOIR AND CONGREGATION.

X. CONCLUDING PRAYER,

PROFESSOR WILLIAM HENRY GREEN, D.D., LL.D.

XI. BENEDICTION,

VICE-CHANCELLOR TELFAIR HODGSON, D.D., LL.D.

XII MUSIC,

POSTLUDE.

ORCHESTRA AND ORGAN.

Committee.

JAMES W. ALEXANDER, A.M., CHAIRMAN.

SAMUEL H. PENNINGTON, M.D., LL.D.,   JOHN A. STEWART, A.M.,
WILLIAM HENRY GREEN, D.D., LL.D.,   CHARLES E. GREEN, A.M.,
WILLIAM M. PAXTON, D.D., LL.D.,   JAMES O. MURRAY, D.D., LL.D.,
E. R. CRAVEN, D.D.,   CHARLES W. SHIELDS, D.D., LL.D.,
ANDREW F. WEST, PH.D.

M. TAYLOR PYNE. LL.B., SECRETARY.

ADDRESS ON BEHALF OF THE COLLEGE.

THERE is but one other Commencement in the history of the college, which may claim an interest as engrossing as that which centres in the Commencement of 1888. It is the Commencement of 1748, first in the lengthening series, held at Newark, Nov. 9th of that year. On the morning of that day, the Trustees, presided over by his Excellency Jonathan Belcher, Governor and Commander in chief of the Province of New Jersey, had unanimously chosen to the Presidency of the College, the Rev. Aaron Burr. The public exercises then began with a solemn prayer of the President elect to God in the English tongue (as the chronicle of the day reports) for a blessing upon the public transactions of the day, upon his majesty King George the Second and Royal family, upon the British Nation and Dominions, * * * and particularly upon the infant College of New Jersey. Then the assembly were called on to stand up and hearken to his Majesty's Royal Charter granted to the Trustees of the College.

The exercises of the afternoon were opened by President Burr, who gave an eloquent oration in the Latin tongue, delivered memoriter. The address, judging from the report made of it to the *Pennsylvania Journal*, is marked by the breadth of its views regarding the province of college education. It recognized the fraternity of American Colleges, by a graceful tribute to Harvard and Yale "which have now flourished for many years, and have sent forth many hundreds of learned men * * * that in different periods have proved the honor and ornament of their Country, and of which the one or the other had been the Alma Mater of most of the Literati then present." The address closed by expressing the conviction that "learning * * * had now begun to dawn upon the Province of New Jersey," and by eulogizing the ample provisions and liberal terms of the Royal

Charter.   Six young scholars were then admitted to the degree of Bachelor of Arts, and among them stood Richard Stockton, a future signer of the Declaration of Independence.   The Trustees completed the business of the day by the adoption of a Corporation Seal.   Its mystic symbolism is thus interpreted.   In the upper part of the circle, a Bible spread open, with Latin characters inscribed on the left side signifying the Old Testament, and on the right side, the New with this motto over it, "Vitæ lumen mortuis reddit."   Underneath on one side a table with books standing thereon to signify the proper business of the student, on the other a diploma with the college seal appended, over it being written "meriti praemium," to signify that the degrees to be conferred are only to those that deserve them.

The principles to govern the future growth of the College were thus fully set forth, as we consider the charter, the first inaugural address, and the college seal, viz: that education here was to be something altogether broader than mere training of godly men for the ministry, and on the other hand that education here was to be in its profoundest sense *Christian*.   By such ties then, are the Commencements of 1748 and 1888, linked together.   The infant College of New Jersey in 1748, having escaped all the ills incident to college childhood—especially its most dangerous foe, want of nourishment—aspires in 1888 to be the University of Princeton.   The life of institutions, as history fully attests, is determined largely, if not absolutely fixed, by the spirit of their founders.   Be that liberal and progressive, the type is there, as the oak in the acorn.   But while this is unquestionably true, we cannot forget that the men who preside over their expansion must be men comprehending fully and in hearty sympathy with, the principles governing their foundation.   Such in fact have been the men who in this country have been chosen to this high office.   The Presidents of our American Colleges have from the beginning been men of noble mark, the very elect in their callings, leaders in the church, not seldom leaders in both Church and State.   No other class of men have done more than they to build up our American civilization which, though according to Mr.

Matthew Arnold, it may not be interesting, seems somehow to have a profound significance for the student of history. Yes, American College Presidents have moulded the life of the State, quite as much as that of the Church. If they have not always been profound scholars, they have been men, whose *characters* educated those under them, for after all it is the force of character in the teacher back of his learning, which is the most powerful factor in his work. The mention of such names as may be found among the presidents of Harvard; of President Dwight of Yale (whose lineal descendant and namesake, holding the same position, graces by his presence our festivities to-day); of Presidents Wayland and Hopkins, is both illustration and proof of this statement. And as I run rapidly over the list of our own College Presidents, it will be seen that the Presidency of the College of New Jersey has been ever held by men of whom any institution might be proud, men who through varying fortune have led the college from its infancy up to the position it holds to-day, at home and abroad.

President Dickinson was the first; in office less than a year, dying untimely in the ripeness of his learning, of great practical wisdom, with every gift to guide successfully the fortunes of the young institution. Succeeded by *President Burr*, who brought to his official work, high powers of organizing and administration, and under whose presidency, the college at once strode to influence, eulogized at his death, by Benjamin Franklin as "a great scholar and a very great man." Then came that greatest of names among American theologians, *Jonathan Edwards*, who by his untimely death, just after induction to office, has left here only the legacy of his illustrious name. After him *Samuel Davies*, that foremost of American preachers, whose monument is seen to-day on our campus, Nassau Hall, miscalled North College, the means for building which he, before his appointment to the Presidency, obtained from friends in England and Scotland: in office only two short years, but wielding a noble and powerful influence in behalf of the College abroad and at home, building his own character into it even in that short time. Next *Samuel Finley*, the man of various learning, an eminent divine, and well described in his epitaph as,

> Artibus, literisque excultus,
> Præ ceteris præcipue enituit,
> Rerum divinarum scientia.

And so in succession *John Witherspoon*, whose services as an American patriot and signer of the Declaration of Independence only bring into more conspicuity, his distinguished administration of the college presidency, and whose Scotch birth proves that men may be born British subjects and yet form American citizens in every fibre of their being. *Samuel Stanhope Smith*, the man of elegant culture, infusing into the college life its refining power, and of whom Washington wrote to his namesake George Washington Custis, sometime a student here, "No college has turned out better scholars, or more estimable characters than Nassau, nor is there any whose president is thought more expert to direct a proper system of education than Dr. Smith." *Ashbel Green*, that born leader in the American Presbyterian Church, the intimate friend of the saintly Bishop White, and whose firm hand the college felt as he took the helm, and who brought to his great work a reputation for theological ability, only second to that for practical energy. *James Carnahan*, sagacious, laborious in executive work, less of the scholar than most of his predecessors, but wise enough to bring into the Faculty such men as Joseph Henry, Stephen Alexander, Albert Dod, John Torrey, Joseph Addison, and James W. Alexander *par nobile fratrum*. *John Maclean*, whose name as I speak it calls up that venerated form so lately vanished from his native town, whose life is one long record of devotion to the college, whose courage and faith stood true in the dark hours of its history, the courtly, benign, beloved, thrice-beloved of teachers and of Presidents. Lastly, and how nobly crowning the succession, *James McCosh*, who would have been famous in philosophy, had he never been President, but whose twenty years in Princeton constitute the most distinguished era in its history.

And to-day we add another, the twelfth of these apostles of learning and religion, President Patton.

In behalf, therefore, of the College; of the Trustees who have chosen you to this high office; of the Faculty heartily approving, sincerely rejoicing in their choice; of the students who admire no less than they prize the many qualities which determined your selection for the post, I bid you, President Patton, our most sincere and enthusiastic welcome. We pledge you our most generous co-operation. We have the proud confidence that you will rise to meet the greater responsibilities of a greater future for Princeton, be it college or university, with triumphant success. And when the Commencement of 1897 dawns on us, as the college shall then have rounded out its century and a half of historic achievement, we are well assured that your administration will have abundantly proved itself the worthiest of successors to the noble lineage of our college presidencies.

ADDRESS ON BEHALF OF THE ALUMNI.

THE task which has been assigned to me to-day is illuminated in my mind by a large and brilliant sense of incompetency to perform it. Old Princeton has more than three thousand living sons, and at least as many daughters-in-law, actual and prospective. What man could hope to utter with sufficient brevity to keep alive the soul of wit, the sentiments with which they regard the accession of a new President to this venerable, renowned, and beneficent institution?

But one thing at least shall not fail in this address. Others could speak more eloquently; none shall speak more warmly and sincerely. Bound by personal gratitude to the grand old man who in our day found Princeton brick and leaves it brownstone, bound by personal friendship to the strong new man whose keen intellect and genial spirit won my boyish admiration in my father's house, I can speak from the heart, in saying to him whose work is crowned *Benedictus,* and to him whose work is inaugurated, *Benedicatur.* And whatever power my voice may lack shall be supplied by many voices saying heartily *Amen.*

The past is completed: it needs no eulogy. The future appears: it needs only a greeting. To you, Sir, in the spirit of hope, all the Alumni of the institution of which you are now the head, offer a sincere and cordial welcome. Welcome! 'Tis a good old word, and we use it for two reasons. We believe that you have come well,—by fair and honorable means,—to this high place. And we believe that it is well that you have come to a position which you promise to fill and to adorn.

Let us rehearse, with due regard to the modesty of President Patton, a few of the reasons for the faith that is in us. Of intellectual qualifications let those speak who have felt the keenness of his lance in philosophic tournament. His adversaries shall praise him in the gates. But we who are his friends, rejoice, first of all, in the conviction, drawn from his own words, that he is an American in spirit, as he will soon be in name. We think little of the accident that he was born out of his native country. It was due to circumstances over which he had no control. It has little bearing upon his nationality. In fact, Sir, you are like the Irishman at Cork who was asked whether he was a native of that county. "For the most part I am," said he. "How is that?" said the judge. "Faix, yer Honor," said Pat, "whin I came here from Limerick me weight was siven stone, and that part o' me is Limerick. But now I'm siventeen stone, and tin stone of it is Cork!" The best part of you is American; and we believe that you will not only keep this college true in its loyal service to our great Republic, but that you will also set an example to its students in the practical discharge of all the duties of good American citizenship.

The Alumni rejoice also in the fact that the new President is a believer in the growth and development of Princeton. We are conservatives; but there comes a time when conservatism is only possible by means of progress. You can only keep what you have got by getting more. Such a time has arrived here. Forty professors are too many for a training-school, and too few for a university. We must either go forward or go backward. The eyes of the new President, like those of his predecessor, are in the front of his head. We shall be glad with him, when the last swaddling-band of an outgrown name drops from the infant, and the "College of New Jersey" stands up straight in the centre of the middle states as the University at Princeton.

This is not possible upon a sectarian basis. But, at least for us, it is only possible upon a distinctly Christian basis. It were better that this institution should close its doors to-morrow than cease to stand inflexibly for Christ and His truth.

Several things are needed before the advancement of Princeton can be accomplished,—larger endowments, more instructors, more fellowships, more students. But there is one thing which we hope will not be forgotten: and that is a stronger allegiance

and a closer corporate spirit among the whole body of the Alumni.
It is doubtful whether this can be developed merely through the
digestive and financial organs,—that is to say by eating annual
dinners and passing the contribution box. At Oxford and Cambridge the graduates are part of the governing body. Harvard,
Yale, Cornell, Amherst, Williams, Brown and other colleges have
called their sons into active partnership in the firm. This seems
essential to the Anglo-Saxon idea of a University. How it is to
be accomplished for Princeton it does not become us to suggest.
We believe that President Patton desires it; and we say to him in
familiar language, "Please now, Sir, bring it out in your own way."

There is one other point on which the utterances of the new
President have given great satisfaction to the Alumni. He is in
favor of Athletics. We do not expect him to make touch-downs
or base-hits, or to enter the arena among the gladiators to

> " pat their brawny arms
> "And stake his sesterces upon their gore."

On the contrary we hope that he will diligently suppress those
gladiatorial features which now dishonor intercollegiate athletics.
But we look to the head of this college to encourage among all
the students those active games in which gentlemen contend with
each other, not for gate-money, prizes, or championships, but for
mutual pleasure and the development of manly courage, patience,
strength and self-control.

None could understand better than yourself, Sir, the ardu-
ous responsibilities and difficulties of your position. How they
are to be met, it is your task to discover and devise. Our chief
desire is that you shall have a free course and full support. When
the vessel is to pass between the Scylla of radicalism and the
Charybdis of reaction, it needs a Ulysses, not as a figure-head at
the bow, but as a helmsman at the stern. The rudder is in your
charge.

Alumni, don't talk to the man at the wheel! Let him steer.
But say "God speed the ship"; and bear a hand; and give a cheer
for Patton the new Pilot of Princeton.

INAUGURAL ADDRESS.

WE listened this morning to the story of "Twenty Years of Princeton," as told by the distinguished President whose administration has just come to a close. Remarkable as that administration would under any circumstances have been, it has been rendered more remarkable by the unique combination of events which coupled the accession of Dr. McCosh to the Presidency of the College, with an outflow of beneficence which has made possible the realization of the comprehensive scheme which he projected in his own inaugural address. During these years Dr. McCosh has been known not only as the wise and energetic administrator of the affairs of Princeton, but as an active force in the educational system of the land. Speaking now only of his services to this institution, it is simple truth to say that he has enlarged its curriculum, elevated its standard of instruction, increased its material resources, and doubled the number of its students. He has given Princeton a proud position as the home of Philosophy, and at the same time has enriched our literature with contributions to mental science which have spread far and wide the fame of this seat of learning, and vindicated for it afresh the place it has always held as a defender of the faith. He has good reason for satisfaction as he reviews the work of these twenty years; and we shall all concede that he has earned the rest from official responsibility which the transfer of office just effected will secure him. We congratulate ourselves upon the fact that he is still with us, and that, as his inclination may lead him or his strength shall allow, he will still take an active part in the instructions of that department of which he has so long been the distinguished head. We are in no danger of forgetting him. We shall never cease to reverence him; and I at least shall claim from time to time the privilege of his advice and the benefit of his experience. I express the feelings of all who are here to-day, and of thousands all over the land, in hoping that he may have a serene old age, and that he may live to see the carrying out in other hands of plans which he himself had formed, and the completion under the direction of another builder of that University-structure that has these years past had ideal existence in his own mind.

It has, I confess, the appearance of hardihood for me to consent, conscious as I am of my own inadequacy for the task, to be Dr. McCosh's successor; and, as some of you know, I hesitated for some time before I felt ready to cross the threshold of the door which was held open to me in my election with such generous and inviting welcome. For I knew my own limitations, and I could not but know that they would be accentuated by being placed in direct antithesis to the shining qualities of my predecessor. I could not hope that my coming into the Presidency would mark a new era of munificence, though it is true that history sometimes repeats itself; and yet I knew that, whether this were so or not, the friends of the College would look for a period of development and growth. If, however, this expectation of growth was enough to make me hesitate to accept the invitation to be the head of this College, a desire for arrested growth or a willingness to remain in a condition of contented stagnation would have made me prompt to decline it. It would be comparatively easy, I suppose, to administer the affairs of this institution if we were willing to occupy a somewhat humble place in the sisterhood of American Universities. With our buildings, our endowments, and our somewhat assured position no very great effort would be needed to keep a certain hold upon the community. But I do not enter upon this work because I am looking for an easy place. I believe that Princeton is only at the beginning of her career, and that her future will as far transcend her present as her present transcends her past. It is at all events under the inspiration of this hope that I enter upon my work to-day. I thank the Trustees for the cordial unanimity with which they have expressed their desire to have me here; I thank my colleagues in the Faculty for the heartiness with which they welcome one of their own number to this honorable position; I need and I am sure that I shall seek the co-operation of both the Trustees and the Faculty in the discharge of my duties; and while it is quite possible that I may not meet their expectations of efficiency, I think that they will have no occasion to complain of my lack of devotion to Princeton College. From this moment onward I shall strive with heart and mind to promote the interests of this institution; and may God give me strength to do for Him the work that my hands find to do.

It would be natural for me to be interested in the growth of the College were it only through the zeal which the existence of competing interests is so apt to enkindle. But I think we should appeal to far higher motives than this in our desire to promote the growth of this institution. Indeed, I begin to fear that we may fall into a state of mind toward our sister colleges which may prevent us from doing full justice to the good work which they are doing and may lead us to forget the common work in which we are engaged. To a certain extent we cannot help being affected by the habits of the business world; but I am nevertheless profoundly of the opinion expressed by Professor Laurie that "pure devotion to science and philosophy is utterly incompatible with the mental disturbance and degradation involved in academic shopkeeping." It is because our educational institutions are making permanent contributions to our American civilization that they are worthy of the best efforts of those who are engaged in their management; and it is because we think that Princeton has an important and a special contribution to make to that civilization that we can heartily wish for her advancement. Local pride, the interest we all feel in our own, and the desire to hold our own in the race for academic pre-eminence may very properly act as subordinate motives; but they are not enough to give strength to sustained endeavor. We must show, if we would make good our claim to the growing confidence of the public, that we are doing a special work for the world.

The relation of the University to the problem of the world's improvement is itself a large question, and one that might well claim consideration if time allowed. That totality of effects in the progress of human life which we call civilization may be viewed both as cause and effect in respect to the higher education. There is a civilization before there is an organized effort to advance it: man improves himself before he begins to to think that he ought to improve himself. Blindly, and as if by instinct, toward ideals that are not consciously placed before him, and through a force that can be likened only to inspiration, he moves on and up. He thinks and reasons, interrogates himself and interprets the world long before he raises questions respecting *a priori* knowledge, and the intelligibility of the universe, or realizes that the answers to these questions determine the possibility of science. Grammar exists before grammarians; logic before logicians construct mood and figure; and civilization takes a long step before it becomes conscious of itself, and begins to plan for its own advancement. When however it reaches this latter stage it invents appliances to promote its own growth. It organizes with more care the institutions of society, and helps Nature to give birth to higher forms of life and thought by establishing the School and the University. Hence it is that the University serves at first to garner and to crystallize results that have been already attained. We can enlarge upon the *trivium* and *quadrivium* of mediæval learning only as in the slow processes of evolution new sciences are born and new departments accepted as solid additions to knowledge. The University itself is sometimes the birth-place of these new sciences, but not always. We can make no contract with nature to secure a monopoly of genius to the guilds of learning. Franklin and Faraday were not academic men. Leibnitz, Des Cartes and Locke did not write in the service of universities. Mill and Spencer have spoken to a wider public than college classes. Equip your university as you may, the extra-mural teacher will always have a place among the factors in our intellectual growth. It may be said in fact that the university is not the mother but the foster-mother of culture. If however it conserves it also promotes civilization. A college is not simply a place for pedants and grammarians; it is a place where the ideas that rule the world find expression. No one knew this better than Hobbes who found in the teaching of the universities the strongest barriers against the success of his own philosophy, and nowhere than in his Leviathan do we accordingly find fuller appreciation of the influence of the university upon the thought and action of a people. It is on account of this influence that our educational institutions deserve the consideration of those who value the world's welfare. For if our real wealth consists not in our corn and wheat, not in our coal-mines and railroads, not in our expensive houses and luxurious modes of locomotion, not in our immunity from toil, and the possession of abundant means of gratifying desire,—but in refined manners, high morals, devout life, cultivated powers, and wide knowledge of men and things: then, behind the agents who make and who execute the laws, behind the people who vote and the machinery by which the popular will is expressed, and back of the avenues of trade along which material wealth rolls up to our doors,—we may well place as having first importance the institutions that represent the best type of moral and intellectual culture; the institutions that by their very genius and constitution stand for and illustrate the best elements of living. The university is intended to be the home of culture, an intellectual retreat, a place where learning keeps state, and where men are interested, as Arnold says, "in things of mind." It is a matter of no small moment to us as a nation to have here and there a place that in a measure at least can give tone to thought, a place where conscience is quickened and taste refined, a place where men not only admire but learn also, as Ste. Beuve says, "why it is right to admire;" a place remote at least in sympathy from the exciting influences of trade, where the bull-fights and bear-fights of commercial speculation are unknown, and where the even tenor of academic life is broken only when some unlucky investor wakes to find that his railroad has passed its dividend or defaulted on its bonds. It is easy of course for the university to fall short of doing its full duty. Learned leisure may become learned indolence, but the university is meant to be a place of endowed research. It is a hive as well as a home. We have not yet reached the full stage of productive activity that is desirable in this land because our professors as a rule are over-worked in the class-room. We have not fully learned the difference between a professor and a pædagogue, and that while the one may hear lessons, the other should inspire with the thirst for knowledge, and speak with authority. But we are coming to this position. We are finding that the professor who has ceased to learn is unfit to teach, and that the man who sees nothing before him to kindle his own enthusiasm will chill the little enthusiasm the student may carry into his lecture-room. There is no necessary antagonism between a man's work as a teacher and his work as an investigator. It is the man who is making contributions to his department whom the students wish to hear. None know this better than Princeton men who remember Professor Henry as the prince of teachers, and who at the same time know that he was the father of telegraphy, and that it is his genius that has enabled us to whisper round the world.

Add now to the civilizing influence that comes through the simple presence of a body of learned men in the different educational centres or that is exerted by these men in published writings, the influence which they exert upon their pupils who take their teachings with them into the various callings of life and reproduce or modify them in the pulpit, on the platform, or through the press: remember that the thought of the world rules the world, and that the best thought ought to rule it: remember too that true views of civilization, of the functions of government, and the basis of law; true answers to the question, how to live and what to live for; high ideals of the fit, the becoming, the beautiful, and the good, are the pillars of national stability,—and we shall see the importance from a national point of view not only or even chiefly of having our universities well-equipped but of having them built upon the right foundations. To be identified with the life of one of these institutions and so to have a hand upon the lever that uplifts the world is a matter of great privilege. I say this not only with respect to professors but with respect to the founders and benefactors of these institutions. And here by the way we are reminded of one of the most remarkable factors of the new-world civilization. The old-world universities are State institutions or they rest upon monastic foundations, or have grown up in obedience to royal mandates. The great colleges of America are for the most part the fruit of private beneficence. I need not speak of those to whom we are indebted here. Their names are household words and we hold them in grateful remembrance. It is in the princely munificence of these men and of men like them connected with other universities, that we see some of the highest achievements of American civilization. This is true even in those cases where we may question the wisdom that directs the benefactions. There are cases where that wisdom may be questioned. A man with a million is not likely to be casting about for an adviser— and yet his will may be misdirected. It has occurred to many that more good would be done—leaving out of sight of course the special claims of new regions of country—if men would give to institutions already established rather than create new ones. A million dollars would make a very meagre university, but half a million would double the efficiency of one already established. To be sure a man who builds his university from the foundation is free from some embarrassing questions; just as a man who has no relations is sure to have no poor relations. But it is a pity not to see that a great past is a priceless thing. Mr. White has recently sketched for us the outline of the next American University. It may be that he is correct and that I am not a disinterested judge, but it seems to me that the question now is not so much what the next university shall be as how the existing universities shall be strengthened. And whether Mr. White be right or wrong in his conception of the ideal American University, we know that Princeton University must conform to the genius of her history and grow along the lines that have been determined by her past. Measured by the years of our sister University of Bologna, that has just celebrated her 8ooth anniversary, we are not old. We remember that Oxford and Cambridge date from the 12th century, that St. Andrews was founded in 1411, that it is 300 years since Rollock presided over the University of Edinburgh, and that it becomes us to take a modest place beside our fair American sister who celebrated her own 250th anniversary only eighteen months ago. But after all age is a relative thing. And when a national institution antedates the national life it has a fair claim to consideration on the ground of age. We have a royal charter: we had a colonial history: the sign-manual of Princeton's President is on America's Magna Charta: and a Princeton graduate helped to make America's Constitution. By burning word and battle-scar our college has won the right to be heard through all the years to come in all that affects the highest interests of Church and State. Independent of both, she has been true to both; and she will be false to her founders and deserve to be deserted by her friends whenever she parts with her patriotism or her piety. I lay emphasis upon both: love of country and love of God, were prominent characteristics of the men who laid the foundations of this institution; and I feel to-day that in both regards the labors of men like Davies and Witherspoon have left a heritage of obligation to me as I take my place in this great succession.

But as in my opinion true patriotism consists not so much in glorying in the victories over a misguided foe as in seeking to foster the virtues that underlie national stability, so I believe that true piety is fostered not so much by a frequent repetition of religious formulas as by a robust avowal of our Christian faith and a manly vindication of it as a reasonable thing. We do not mean to extinguish the torch of science that we may sit in religious moonlight, and we do not intend to send our religion up to the biological laboratory for examination and approval. We shall not be afraid to open our eyes in the presence of Nature, nor ashamed to close them in the presence of God. And here the truth of history requires me to say that it is only in a qualified sense that the Log College can be called the mother of Princeton University. The Log College, like the College of New Jersey, had its origin in the noble desire of devout and God-fearing men to promote Christian education, and while it is proper in view of all the facts, as Dr. Alexander shows, to speak of the Log College as the germ of the College of New Jersey, it must also be remembered that the latter had an independent beginning, and that while the Log College was meant to meet the religious exigencies of the time by making a shorter road into the Christian ministry, the College of New Jersey was from the beginning in the intentions of its founders a seat of learning. The conditions under which Princeton has grown to its present position must be the law of its future development. Said President Green: "It is hoped that the guardians of Nassau Hall will forever keep in mind, that the design of its foundation would be perverted if religion should ever be cultivated in it to the neglect of science; or science to the neglect of religion; if on the one hand it should be converted into a religious house like a monastery or Theological Seminary in which religious instruction should claim almost exclusively the attention of every pupil: or upon the other hand should become an establishment in which science should be taught how perfectly soever, without connecting with it and constantly endeavoring to inculcate the principles and practice of piety. Whatever other institutions may exist or arise in our country in which religion and science may be separated from each other by their instructors or governors, this institution without a gross perversion of its original design can never be one." These words I make my own to-day, and, so help me God, during the time of my administration, Princeton shall keep faith with the dead.

If, then, we are seeking to comprehend our position among the higher institutions of learning in our land, we must keep our history in view. It is well known that, in the judgment of many, the time has come for Princeton College to assume the name and style of a University. The exigencies of the hour, therefore, require me to ask what a university is, and what kind of a university Princeton is to be? It is not as easy as some suppose to to distinguish the college from the university by sharp boundary lines. It will not do to say that college and university in America correspond to gymnasium and university in Germany, for the

German gymnasium is not exactly the same as the American college, and the German university is only one of several forms of university organization. It would be easy to theorize with respect to what the American university ought to be; or if the American university were defined by State or Federal laws and were possessed of definitely recognized privileges and charter rights that distinguish it from a college, we might say what the American university actually is. When, however, in the absence of material for determining what the American university is, we ask the more general question regarding the marks of a university, we must fall back upon the historical usage of the word as illustrated in the recognized universities of the world. That usage shows that some of the prevailing views upon this question are erroneous. It is said, for instance, that a university is an institution consisting of the four Faculties—Arts, Law, Medicine and Theology, and I confess a certain regard for this traditional idea, though I see that there is no logic of exclusion that should limit the learned professions to three, or prevent us from giving university status to other callings. But I deny that it is of the essence of a university to have four Faculties, or even a plurality of Faculties. There was a university at Salerno with only a Faculty of Medicine; Bologna was a university when it gave instruction only in Law; Paris had a university that consisted of a Faculty of Theology. If, then, a university may consist of one Faculty, and of that history leaves us no room to doubt, it may certainly consist of that Faculty which, according to Du Bois Reymond, is the centre of the university system, and which more than any other is concerned with pure science and is least burdened with utilitarian conditions. If a Faculty of Medicine may be a university, a Faculty of Philosophy may surely be one. And what is a well equipped college like this but a Faculty of Philosophy? It is thought by some, however, that it is of the essence of a university that the Faculty of Arts should offer a wide range of studies and that the students should be free in selecting them. But inasmuch as no university professes to teach the *omne scibile*, and as no one has said how closely an institution must approximate

that before arrogating to itself the name of a university, it may
be fairly said that an institution with say forty professors in the
Faculty of Arts, has some claim to the title. The freedom of the
students, however, is only a relative freedom after all, for since
no institution has yet gone so far as to give its degree to students
without imposing some conditions, either of residence or examination, and as to the latter of the kind and number of subjects
professed, it cannot be said that the freedom of the student is an
article of the standing or falling university. It is further said
that the university is to be regarded merely as an examining and
degree-granting body, in some cases having one or more colleges
affiliated with it. This is the prevailing view in England, the idea
growing perhaps out of the relation of the University of Oxford to
its colleges, though as a matter of fact the University antedated
the colleges. The new Victoria University, with its affiliated
colleges of Manchester and Liverpool, is based upon this idea,
and so is that of London. This scheme accomplishes several
good purposes. It limits the number of degree-granting bodies,—
a very good thing to do—secures a high type of impartial exam-
iners, and makes it possible to give the same university rank to
several contiguous institutions without in any way interfering with
their separate autonomies. But as Mr. Lyte says in his History
of Oxford University, speaking of this and a previously given
definition, "Neither will stand the test of history, for there have
been great and learned universities neither professing to impart
universal knowledge nor boasting a single affiliated college."
Omit the scheme of affiliated colleges from the last named conception of the university and we have an approximation to the
University of France, which was, perhaps, in the mind of Mr.
White when he pictured for the readers of *The Forum* the next
University of America. Once more it is thought that the function
of the university is to promote original research and be the resort
of specialists. This is the basis of the German University, and
the nearest approach to it in this country is the Johns Hopkins.
This idea was apparently in the mind of Bacon, as Professor
Laurie reminds us, and the realization of it is, in the judgment of

Professor Ladd, to constitute the American University of the future. There is place, of course, for such a university, but unless we are ready to follow Mr. Arnold and call Oxford a high school, or Mr. Ladd in disparaging the Scotch Universities, as I do not feel disposed to do, we must conclude that the *genus* University exists under several *species*. There are no principles of induction known to me that will justify us in taking any one of these as the type of the real university. History seems to teach us that we may use this word with a great deal of liberty, and until legislation has defined its use and limited its application, we may expect to hear of institutions that use this trade-mark without rising to our standard of what a university ought to be. Professor Laurie gives us three "notes" of a university, and I am willing to take them on his authority, partly because they give me the opportunity to say that however the question regarding a change of title may be settled—and on that subject I have no opinion to express— Princeton is already a university, if there ever was a university in the world; and partly also because these three notes of a university will furnish the basis for a word or two regarding the management of Princeton College that may not be out of place on this occasion. The three notes of a university referred to are *studium generale*, Freedom and Autonomy. The *studium generale* has a double reference, being intended to mean both a place of general resort for students, and a place where liberal studies are pursued. The *studium generale* was not a monks' school designed to fit men for the priesthood, but a school intended for all who choose to frequent it. Realize the non-ecclesiastical character of the university, and its other attributes follow by logical consequence.

The founders of the College of New Jersey organized it upon this university basis. They were religious men; they were Presbyterians; but with a breadth of view not surprising when we remember who they were, they planted the institution on a broad basis of a *studium generale*. Says the late President Maclean: "Either the superior judgment of those concerned in the foundation of our college or their great liberality of sentiment, or else the circumstances of their position, perhaps all combined, led them to adopt the very best plan possible for the right founding and right ordering of such an institution. They made it neither a State college nor a Church college, but committed it to the oversight and care of a select number of the very best men interested in their enterprise and who had the confidence and respect of the whole community, being leading men in both Church and State." They planned their college for liberal culture. Their charter imposes no religious tests upon professors, and it expressly provides that none shall be imposed upon the students. The founders of the college planned, therefore, for academic freedom, which is also a note of the university. Organize an institution, not as a propaganda, but as a seat of learning; make your professors servants of Truth and your students seekers of it, and freedom is the necessary result. The scientific man will ask, what say the facts, not what says the creed. The student of politics will ask, what is best, not what the platform is. He may not vote with Gladstone or Salisbury. He may be neither a Democrat nor a Republican. He may glory in his independence and be reactionary or revolutionary, or he may represent the resolution of forces in the compromising diagonal, bear the opprobrium of an ill-sounding designation, but feel sure, nevertheless, that the "Mugwump" has his reward: he is free. He may abuse his freedom, and glory rather in his emancipation than in the advantage that emancipation brings him, and stand opposed to the old order of things for the sake of showing that he is free. This is freedom with some of freedom's excesses. We hear much just now of university freedom. Kant advocated it a hundred years ago, and Helmholtz sounded its praises in 1877. I believe in freedom, but in concrete experience we must take note of the qualifications of freedom. The genius of the university is freedom, but the genius of such a university as this is a qualified freedom. The trustees have responsibilities; so have the professors. These limit freedom. We have no scientific confession of faith, but we would not let a Communist teach political economy, nor Mr. Jasper astronomy; we would not give academic standing to the "Substantial Philosophy" of Mr. Wilford Hall, nor permit one of the Flat-Land people to instruct in physical geography; we would not allow Mr. Sinnett to teach Esoteric Buddhism, or entertain a class with Madam Blavatsky's vagaries, because we believe in the freedom of philosophizing. We should also close our doors to the crude idealism professed by the so-called Christian scientists and the metaphysical healers. It is no part of university freedom to shelter nonsense or give learned leisure to the charlatan. Nor is it part of university freedom to open the halls of science and philosophy to men who teach atheism or belittle the Christian faith. I am not sure that I should commit myself to all the propositions in Virchow's famous "Ignorabimus" speech, though I am in sympathy with its main ideas; and I have no difficulty in saying that on the general question under discussion I stand with him rather than Haeckel, his great antagonist. Limitations may be similarly shown to exist with regard to the students' freedom. A wise man recognizes the difference between adolescence and infancy. A wise man knows better than to treat a grown man like a child. What laws we need in college will depend on circumstances. Put your university in a city having no students in residence and the municipal authorities will take care of the discipline. Put five hundred men in residence and regulations become necessary. What regulations are necessary is a matter of time, place and circumstances. Self-government is ideal government. Spontaneous obedience to a self-imposed law that supersedes law imposed by another is ideal life. I fear it will take at least another administration to bring the Princeton undergraduate up to that standard.

Autonomy, not of the individual, however, but of the institution, is the third note of a university. The mediæval University was a guild of learning. Its autonomy and its privileges went together. It could hold property, manage its own affairs, and punish its members. It possessed valuable franchises. It was supreme in its region. They were protectionists in those mediæval days; but they were also fair. They would not have thought it right to give letters patent to the inventor of a lamp-chimney and let the poor scholar burn his midnight oil for the sole bene-fit of thankless and unremunerating publishers. No university could sell learning without a charter. And when we add the social consideration that the University had, and the political power that it afterwards came to have, we can see that it was a great matter for it to have its privileges and its autonomy to-gether. We have autonomy without the privileges. There is little in common between our autonomy and that of the mediæval University, except the independence of Church and State. A university ought not to be bound by party politics or sectarian Theology. A Theological Seminary, however, though its Pro-fessors are engaged in the highest kind of university work, as in the case of our own Seminary here that has done so much for Princeton's world-wide fame, ought to be under the supervision of the church whose theology it represents. The entire distinct-ness as to end and organization of the two great institutions that live side by side in this place and in such close relations is mani-fest at once. And now the question arises whether the autonomy of the College might not be modified to advantage. Should we not seek to realize a literary republic? Should we not seek to give form to the solidarity of university life? Some think that there is too great a barrier between Professors and Trustees; others that the graduates ought to have their interests stimulated through more tangible ideas than filial piety and a love for Alma Mater. It is felt by some that college administration is a business in which Trustees are the partners, Professors the salesmen, and Students the customers; and it is said that university life would take a great step forward if without interference with existing relations, many of which cannot be changed, there might never-theless be a common ground on which the representatives of the different interests could meet for consultation and action.

These are questions that are likely to be presented to the consideration of universities in this and other lands. They are questions respecting which I should be slow to speak and where I shall more willingly follow than attempt to lead. And yet with-

out offense I trust I may venture to exercise the academic imagination, and picture to myself the state of things that may perhaps
exist in Princeton—say a hundred years to come—when on some
ceremonial occasion like the present a University Convocation
shall assemble. The University Senate is in session, let me first
suppose. The Trustees of Princeton College are there, and representatives of the College Faculty are members of it; distinguished
men from the Faculty of Theology add the weight of their wise
opinion; the Faculty of Law has a representative; and representatives of the Alumni speak for their brother graduates all around
the world. It is an august body composed of men who represent
high character, practical sagacity, great and varied learning,
profound thought, high position and refined culture. They sit
in consultation on purely academic questions—the granting of
degrees, the enlargement of the curriculum, or the importance of
establishing a University Professorship in Comparative Religion,
or Christian Archæology, or the Institutes of Public Law. And
now as in imagination I see the robed procession of Senate,
Faculties, Fellows, Graduates and Undergraduates enter the
Commencement Hall, I cannot resist the feeling that we have
made a great advance in our academic life; that we have put
into incarnate form, ideas that even now float vaguely in the
minds of some; and that impressions have taken organic shape
that are already prevalent across the sea, regarding Princeton
University.

It is however a more practical question which concerns us
now: and having vindicated our title to university rank, I trust
you will bear with me if I go on to say what kind of University
Princeton ought to be. I believe that the learning acquired at
a university should be regarded as valuable for its own sake
rather than for the sake of the use that is to be made of it.
That being the case while we would not preclude professional
training it will naturally take a subordinate place in our plans,
and our idea regarding the aim of a university will be a restraining
influence in relation to the development of schools that teach
men the material arts. Much, too, that often passes for academic

instruction may be ruled out as having no disciplinary value. Mere information, mere lists of names and knowledge of interesting facts is not education. "Stuffing birds," as Newman says, "and playing on stringed instruments is an elegant pastime and a resource 'to the idle, but it is not education; it does not form or cultivate the intellect." When therefore a new department is proposed, you may expect me to require its advocates to show cause why it should not be excluded on the ground that it has no disciplinary value. Moreover the general training of men for their career in life must be our first consideration. Original research is a luxury for the few. The many feel about it as Locke did about poetry, " 'Tis a pleasant land but a barren soil." Guided then by the principle just stated we may study the problem of Princeton's curriculum. We have two departments, the academic and the scientific. In the latter the tendency to provide professional education has found expression in the course in civil engineering, and I should favor a further development of the professional side of the School of Science, provided always it be kept in mind that pure science with a practical outlook, rather than practical business on a scientific basis is our plan of education. It is, however, on the academic side of the College that the main discussions regarding the curriculum are going on both here and elsewhere. We have in the first place the old fashioned college curriculum of four years, prescribed throughout. There can be no question of the high quality of the work that has been done in the past and that many colleges are still doing on this basis. It gives a good preparation for professional and specialized study. But it does not do justice to the special aptitudes of students and it necessarily excludes some very important branches of study. Next to this is the plan that allows the student to choose for himself out of a very extended curriculum what studies he will pursue. With the best students this may possibly produce the best results, though even regarding them we may well ask with Mr. Lowell whether it is, "indeed, so self-evident a proposition as it seems to many that 'you may' is as wholesome a lesson as 'you must.'" Once more it is said that the College course should be regarded as equivalent to the instruction given in the German Gymnasium and that it should be followed by three or four years in the University. This would practically result in a blotting out of. the Philosophical Faculty in the University, or rather there would be room for only one or two Faculties of this sort—that of Johns Hopkins, for example. The same effect would follow if the standard of admission to college were raised so that men should matriculate only when they had covered the studies included in the Freshman and Sophomore years. They would go as many are now going from the higher academies directly into the professional schools. This by the way is something that should be considered by those who are advocating a higher standard of matriculation. A fourth plan consists in keeping the college course substantially as it is, modified perhaps by electives in the Junior and Senior years, and distinguishing by the name of University work the studies that are pushed forward into graduate courses. This looks to me too much like building the academic structure with four stories and an attic, and putting the University in the attic. It accommodates, to be sure, the number who desire to pursue the higher studies, but the name is too big for the slight use that it serves. There remains then what is substantially our own method which, it seems to me, is admirably suited to the particular work that we are called upon to do. According to this scheme, two years are devoted to a prescribed course of disciplinary study. The two remaining years are devoted to studies partly obligatory and partly optional. There will be a tendency undoubtedly to widen the area of electives in the Junior and Senior years, which however restrained will nevertheless in all probability make necessary some change in the curriculum. It is doubtful whether the scientific professors can do their best work with those who wish to prosecute scientific study unless some of the elements of science are taught in the Freshman and Sophomore years. There is no reason why Logic, being a purely formal science, should not, at least so far as the old Aristotelian logic of deduction is concerned, be taught earlier in the course leaving the higher branches of the study involving metaphysical inquiries until a later stage. I doubt whether we can do what we ought to do in Latin and Greek until we distinguish in the first years of study between pass and honor work, and allow those whose aptitudes are for the humanities opportunity for a more exclusive devotion to them when approaching the close of the college curriculum. For I believe with Mr. Lowell that "Language should be a ladder to literature, and not literature a ladder to language." I would not have less philology, but more light and sweetness in the study of the classics. Some of us love our Milton though we do not read him in the way that Ruskin says we should, and cultivated men value their Latin or Greek as the basis of their literary culture who have no desire to be philological specialists. Hence though Ritschl and Mommsen, as Mr. Roby says, "know more of the Duellian inscription than Quintilian," it is Quintilian and not Ritschl that they will prefer to read. I hope that we shall not forget to read the classics, whether Latin, Greek or English, in our eagerness to read what critics say about them. I hope that the scientific study of literature will not destroy our love of literature, or lead us to forget that its function is to please. I hope that in these days of original research, and when a man must do homage to King Arithmos if he would be great in science, or unearth a new fact by diving into some forgotten closet, if he would stand among the immortals who have done what they call original work, we shall not forget that there is still a place for literary art, that form and grace, that wealth of allusion and easy intellectual pose still count for something in education. Hence I hope that we shall increase our facilities for knowing the resources of our own language, and that the literatures of Italy and Spain will be open to those who wish to read them.

Far be it from me, however, to have literature cultivated at the expense of science. Philosophy and science are to give us the poetry of the future. What is "In Memoriam" but crystalized philosophy? But for Tennyson's knowledge of the forms and processes of modern thought, we should never have had those "jewels five-words long that on the outstretched finger of time sparkle forever." What to the common mind is the dull carbon of dry metaphysics, in the hands of this great lapidary is cut into the gleaming facets of the diamond. Philosophy sits as queen among the sciences and we see her dressed in her robes of state when we turn to the pages of Tennyson and Browning.

I am speaking therefore in the interest of literature when I commend the study of science and philosophy. And as I am speaking of literature let me speak on a subject that lies on the border-land of literature. I shall be sorry for Literature when History accepts a Fellowship in the Royal Society, and I shall be sorry for History when she is deserted by literary artists, and when we who do but read her annals must encounter the dust of the state-paper office. Nevertheless it is as science or rather as philosophy that History should be taught. I have no desire to see numerous courses of lectures on History form part of our curriculum and allowed to count as elective studies. For if this method be adopted there would be no reason why such courses should not be multiplied indefinitely. History can be made an easy study and as it becomes easy it ceases to be discipline, and therefore ceases to perform its proper function in University training. But history studied as Freeman would have it studied is not easy. I believe that Seeley is right in saying that history is to be treated philosophically. The march of events must be rubricised under some conception: shall it be Comte's or Hegel's; Buckle's or Schelling's; or shall we stand with Augustine and Bunsen, with Kingsley and Lilly, and see in the logic of events the thought of God? It is from the experience of the past that we are to gather the canons of to-day. History in this way takes its place in a group of studies which—using the words in its large Aristotelian sense—we may call the Science of Politics. As in Ethics we deal with human conduct with reference to the individual, so in Politics we consider it with reference to society. I think that the first thing to be done in the development of Princeton College is the full equipment of this department of politics. There is room for the specialist in Political Economy, and I could hope that some day we may have a chair exclusively devoted to it; unless Political Economy should be absorbed in the larger department of Social Science as some of the Physical Sciences are absorbed in Biology. It is manifest that as our life grows more complex, new questions will arise; and new problems requiring profound investigation and needing better treatment than they get at the hands of uneducated men with good motives, or educated men with false premises will demand attention. In the interests of national integrity it is important that they shall be dealt with in our colleges; and that our graduates who whatever their calling may be will have the influence as citizens that is accorded to learning, should have a training that will enable them to deal with these problems by taking hold of the philosophical principles that underlie them. I hope that Social Science at no distant day will have an able representative in our Faculty.

I should like also to see some provision made for instruction in the History and Philosophy of Jurisprudence. I am not thinking of a professional law school, though even that may come later. It will be said, perhaps, that the study of Roman law will not help a man to try cases. I have no right to an opinion on that question. But I know that the man who understands the history of jurisprudence, who knows something about the Pandects, or has looked into Gaius and Ulpian, the man who has read Austin and Amos and Holland and Maine and Pollock and Lorimer, to say nothing of Savigny and Stahl, will go to the study of Coke and Blackstone, Story and Greenleaf, Washburn and Parsons a broader man, and that he will be a better jurist if not a better advocate. I believe, too, that in this field of philosophical jurisprudence there is a comparatively unoccupied field, so far as American colleges are concerned, and both for the additions that may be made to Princeton's fame, as well as for the contribution to general culture that would result from the establishment of such a chair, I hope for its foundation. It has been my habit year by year to recommend the students of theology to take advantage of their opportunities to study jurisprudence, and I have the satisfaction of knowing that some of them have profited by my advice. It does a man no harm to be trained in the logic of law; and it is of no little advantage to the clergyman to read the jural language of St. Paul in the light of Roman law, to learn that the testamentary idea originated in the Roman mind, to see what the *jus civile* has done for Christianity, to learn how law in great measure gave form to theological literature, and how in the mellow light of cathedral windows the marriage of jurisprudence and theology was effected. Law is science, Mr. Langdell says, and he teaches it in Harvard by requiring his students to ascertain its rules by induction from leading cases. Law is also philosophy, and its rules rest on principles which it is the task of the philosophical historian to investigate. I hope that Princeton will do justice to her position in philosophy by dealing with this great department of life under philosophical rubrics.

I shall hope also that Philosophy, strictly so-called, will continue to occupy the place in this institution which it has always had, and which has especially been given to it during the administration of Dr. McCosh. I say this not simply because I think it would be a pity for Princeton to lose any of her philosophical prestige, but also because I believe that all interests centre in Philosophy. Everything that we hold dear in faith is involved in the maintenance of the *a priori* elements of knowledge. All departments of inquiry are interested in a right theory of knowledge. We are neither Hegelians nor Comtists. We believe in experience, but we believe in the categories that condition the possibility of experience. Our intuitionalism unifies all our studies, whether they be in the region of science or literature, of history or politics, of jurisprudence or art. It is but natural that I should hope for a reinforcement as soon as practicable of the department of philosophy. And as I shall be more closely related to the philosophical department than any other, I may be pardoned if I say a word regarding it. No department of College instruction should be handled with greater care than this: there is none where it is possible to do greater mischief. If a man goes wrong here he goes wrong everywhere. I shall feel bound to watch jealously the instruction in this department. And yet I shall advocate—in the interests of truth and sound learning—the expansion of this department. The hope of sound philosophy is in seeing to it that sound philosophers are not behind the times. The peril of having eyes is that they may lead us astray; but we cannot afford to put them out. If we are to study philosophy we must use and scrutinize philosophical systems. The books in our Library are meant to be read. We do not keep a philosophical museum where visitors are kindly requested not to handle the specimens. I think that we should prosecute the study of what is erroneously called the new psychology. I have less interest than some in laboratory work in the study of the mind, and I do not grow enthusiastic over diagrams that represent the daily fluctuations of "the normal knee-jerk;" but I believe that we should take advantage of all the light that physiology throws upon the problems of the mind. I do not think that Hegel has said the last word in philosophy; but I do not believe that we should ignore his influence, which, though it be an evil, is yet not an unmitigated evil. Dr. McCosh has been too independent himself to expect or even to desire his successors in the chair of psychology to accept every statement he has made. Yet I believe that in regard to the main points of his contention his position is not only true but vitally related to all truth. And I furthermore believe that nothing will more readily lead to an acknowledgment of this than a discriminating study of the history of philosophy. I should give a very high place to this study in our curriculum. Nothing tends to quicken a man's power of thought more than the critical study of the history of philosophical opinion, and it is more important after all to think than to know "the time it takes to think."

It is to be hoped that the Art Building will commend itself to friends who will secure its speedy completion, and that all requisite instructors in that department will be provided. We do not mean to establish a Conservatory of Music or a School of Painting. Our purpose is to promote æsthetic philosophy by lectures on the History of Art and Archæology, and for such lectures there is an important place in a college curriculum, that aims to be comprehensive.

With these additions to our curriculum, it would be necessary to make some new adjustments, at least in the Senior year, regarding the choice of electives. As far as my present light goes I see no better way than that of allowing a man at the close or toward the middle of his Junior year to proceed to his degree along any of several roads; these roads being indicated roughly by Literature, Science and Philosophy, each being again divided into parallel paths—as that of philosophy might be into pure philosophy, political science, and jurisprudence. There would be difficulties of a practical kind about the group-system and some concessions should be made to those who raise them, but such a system would accomplish several results. It would secure thorough acquaintance with a related group of studies. It would be a protection against the evil effects of scattering the energies over too many fields. It would, therefore, make the Bachelor's degree significant of real education.

Such a system would naturally be arranged according to the analogy of the course of graduate studies that now lead to the degree of Doctor of Science and Doctor of Philosophy, and would be the best preparation for them. To the degree of B.D. and Ph.D., which we now give, we might add, as soon as adequate provision is made for courses in jurisprudence, the degree of LL.B., the doctorate in both Divinity and Law remaining an honorary degree as at present. I trust that these graduate courses will be developed from year to year and that an increasing number of graduates will avail themselves of them. To this end it is greatly to be desired that the University Fellowships, the object of which is to encourage specialized study on the part of graduates, should be added to as rapidly as possible. We have now the names of ten Fellows on our catalogue. It would add incalculably to the efficiency of the college, were it in nothing but the stimulus it would give to undergraduate study, if we had fifty Fellows in attendance every year engaged in advanced work in the several departments of inquiry. And lest some shall sup-

pose that a fellowship is a premium put upon learned leisure, let
me say that the men who are likely to apply for fellowships are
men who, for the most part, will make teaching their profession.
There is a growing demand for training teachers. I think it will
be a good thing for the higher education in this country when it
becomes fully understood that a professor can secure full equipment for his work in the larger colleges of our own land.

On the grounds already given I have taken it for granted
that Princeton is a University. Into the question regarding a
change of name I do not propose to enter. It is a matter that
when the time comes will be wisely dealt with, and I doubt not
that some who hear me to-day will feel that without challenging
my position it would be unwise to make any change in our corporate title before some further advance has been made in the
development of the institution, and doubtless there is great force
in this view. I have indicated in a general way the line of progress which seems to be before the College, and in making the
suggestions that I do I am but acting in the spirit as I suppose
of Dr. McCosh's administration. I have indicated some of the
educational advantages that students enjoy and ought to enjoy
in Princeton. I may, therefore, very properly in my closing
words speak with more special reference to the students themselves. We shall never let a student leave Princeton, if we can
help it, for lack of accommodation, so long as there is a room to be
rented in the town; the students however would prefer to live in a
College Hall, and we should prefer to have all of them do so; but
until we can get a new dormitory that is out of the question.
We shall never let a worthy student go away from Princeton
through lack of ability to pay his tuition fees; and it not uncom-
monly happens that the brightest and best men, the men who
give greatest promise of usefulness and stand at the head of their
classes, find it hard to meet the necessary expenses even when
tuition is remitted, and tuition is remitted every year to the
amount of about $15,000. This is offset by the income of $5,000
from scholarships, and the College is thus giving away every year
about $10,000 in free tuition. We have seventy-two scholarships

of $1,000 each. We need one hundred more. We do not teach our students to spend £1,000 a year, as Sir Lyon Playfair says the English universities do, and I fear that we cannot always teach them to make £1,000 a year as the same gentleman says the Scotch universities do. We may find it difficult sometimes to cultivate literature on a little oatmeal; but I am able to say, after careful inquiry, that a man of moderate means need not hesitate to send his sons to Princeton. We have no wish to make a Princeton degree a rich man's luxury. Our students come mainly from the Middle States. Some come from the West, and some will, continue to come I hope, notwithstanding the growth of the colleges that are doing such admirable work in that region. With the establishment of State universities in the South we may expect that Southern students for the most part will seek their education nearer home: but there are many living under those southern skies who remember "Old Princeton" as their Alma Mater; and I would like to say to them to-day, since "the war drums beat no longer and the battle flags are furled," that it is the same old Princeton that now invites them with their sons to revisit the academic homestead.

Sir Alexander Grant reminds us that when we use the word "college" as distinct from the word "university," the idea of a family, a home, attaches especially to the former word. In this sense we do not wish to outgrow the term. A man misses much of college education who lives in the city and rides to lectures on the street car. Men thrown together in residence educate one another, as Newman says. An education thus obtained is quite as valuable in its way as that derived from the text-book or the lecture. The English universities make gentlemen, Huber says: I would have a university do more than that, but that is not a little thing to do. I hope that besides doing this, the effect of under-graduate life in Princeton is to cultivate the character and foster a manly spirit. I think we give a mental training here that will fit men to do their work in life with credit and success. Those who love study have ample opportunities to gratify their desires; and those who do not love it are under constraining influences. I do not think that either the phrensy of amusements or the phrensy of examinations of which Mr. Freeman speaks, exists among us in a form sufficiently aggravated to distract the minds of serious men. We have idle men, to be sure, and if we could put implicit confidence in Mr. Mahaffy who when speaking of Des Cartes lets fall the statement that "a great deal of idleness is indeed the condition of the highest and the most lasting diligence," we might be looking by and by for some epoch-making books from men who as undergraduates cannot be said to be spoiling their future by premature and excessive mental application. There is however a great deal of hard and high-class work done by our undergraduates. It is a mistake to suppose that our students come only for athletics. This, by the way, is a subject of recognized difficulty in college management. The evils connected with athletics should be checked, but I should be sorry to lose the lessons of manliness that athletics teach. Let us remember what Helmholtz says: "The more young men are cut off from fresh air and from the opportunity of vigorous exercise, the more induced will they be to seek an apparent refreshment in the misuse of tobacco and intoxicating drinks." The gymnasium has my vote as an agent in moral reform.

I ought to say moreover that there is a strong religious influence exerted in Princeton College. The exercises in Murray Hall are a marked feature of College life. It deserves to be said moreover that although the matter of giving Biblical instruction in Colleges is only now beginning to excite attention in some quarters, it has never been neglected here. I should be sorry if I could not hope that my influence upon the College might tend in some degree to strengthen Christian faith and foster Christian life.

I am reminded, as I speak, of the manifold relations I sustain and of the various forms of obligation imposed upon me by the official connection that has been formed to-day between the college and myself. For I shall owe a duty not to students only, but to all the interests that are represented in the college. I desire my relations to the students to be fruitful of the best results, and, therefore, I wish to know them individually and count them my personal friends. I shall hope as year by year they go out to join their fellow-alumni, scattered over the world, to follow them as far as possible with a personal interest in their career, and as my predecessor has done with such conspicuous success, to keep the great body of the graduates interested in the progress of their Alma Mater by telling them of our affairs and how we do, when from time to time the pleasure is afforded me of sharing the hospitalities of their annual reunions. In taking up my work I know that I have much to learn regarding the institution of which I know so much already. I count it one of my special causes for gratification that I shall be able to fall back from time to time upon the wise counsel of the Dean of the College, who has rendered services of priceless value to this institution, and who I am sure will give me the advantage of his large experience in the way that an old friendship will suggest. I shall not cease to be a professor by becoming the President of the College: and I must be allowed to magnify my office and to have the same zeal for my department that my colleagues in the faculty have for their's. I owe it to myself to see to it that my occupancy of this place does not operate to the disadvantage of those qualities which suggested my elevation to it. I should soon demonstrate my unfitness for this position were I to lose my hold upon those departments of study to which I have heretofore given attention. I am encouraged in the feeling that a man may hold a book in one hand and the reins of government in the other when I remember that Dr. Wayland, Dr. Woolsey, Dr. Hopkins and Dr. McCosh, who certainly will always rank among the great College Presidents of America, found time amid the pressure of administrative duties to publish treatises and act as leaders of thought. I believe, however, that the Trustees do not think it necessary for me to promise them that I will not neglect my studies. They, perhaps, are waiting for some evidence that they have not seated a mere book-worm in the Presidential chair, and I beg to say that I will furnish that at my earliest convenience.

True culture culminates in religion. True philosophy has God as its postulate; true science reaches God as its conclusion.

The education therefore that is to prove a valuable element in civilization cannot afford to be indifferent to the claims of divine truth. The best Christians are the best citizens. Without faith in the next world we shall soon lose interest in this. It is not enough, therefore, that we seek to train men who are skilled in mathematics, and cultivated in the knowlege of the great literatures of the world. It is not enough that we be abreast of the times in regard to the great inductions of science or that our professors are well-read in the latest utterances of German philosophy. It is not enough that we maintain no hostile attitude to religion, and that we teach men to think on the great problems of the social economy without prejudice to their hereditary beliefs. It is not enough that we have Christian services on Sunday and that ample accommodations are furnished those who by taste and training are disposed to engage in concerted effort to promote a wholesome religious sentiment in the College. There should be distinct, earnest, purposeful effort to show every man who enters our College Halls the grounds for entertaining those fundamental religious beliefs that are the common heritage of the Christian world. The necessary effect of education is that of awakening the spirit of inquiry on all subjects. And we have no right to conduct a course of study the object of which is to tell a man to think, to induce a man to think, to train a man to think; and the effect of which is a tendency at least to bring the naive convictions of childhood before the bar of reason, that they may show cause why they should not be abandoned—without at the same time doing something to strengthen faith, and give it a reasoned position. I am happy to say that this matter has always been attended to here: and I can only add that if I can do any thing in the pulpit or the lecture-room, by spoken word or printed page, in the formality of professorial instruction or the informality of friendly talk, to strengthen the hands of my colleagues who are already engaged in the work of religious instruction, I shall consider the opportunity of doing so one of the supreme privileges of my position. I believe in the education that fits men not only for life but for eternal life. And so believing I commit myself to the guidance of God, and commend this College to his grace, entreating that during the time that I shall serve it as in former years this seat of learning alike in the work that it may do for science and the witness that it may bear to revealed truth may promote the kingdom of our Lord and Saviour Jesus Christ, to whom be glory ever-more.

www.ingramcontent.com/pod-product-compliance
Lightning Source LLC
Chambersburg PA
CBHW032136080426
42733CB00008B/1091